STICKHORSE SCRIPTURES

HOLY BIBLE

Maureen T. McGinn

WestBow Press books may be ordered through booksellers or by contacting:

WestBow Press
A Division of Thomas Nelson & Zondervan
1663 Liberty Drive
Bloomington, IN 47403
www.westbowpress.com
844-714-3454

Interior Image Credit: Maureen T. McGinn

Scripture quotations are taken from the New American Standard Bible®, Copyright © 1960, 1962, 1963, 1968, 1971, 1972, 1973, 1975, 1977, 1995 by The Lockman Foundation. Used by permission.

ISBN: 978-1-6642-8408-1 (sc)
ISBN: 978-1-6642-8409-8 (hc)
ISBN: 978-1-6642-8407-4 (e)

Library of Congress Control Number: 2022921302

Print information available on the last page.

WestBow Press rev. date: 12/17/2022

WESTBOW
P R E S S®
A DIVISION OF THOMAS NELSON
& ZONDERVAN

DEDICATION:

To my folks who raised me with a strong moral compass and gave me my beginning knowledge of God! For that I am eternally grateful.

INTRODUCTION:

To all the "Guardians" of children everywhere.

When you read this beautifully illustrated book of God's commandments, to the innocent children in your care, know that God placed this book in your hands as a tool to help explain His truths for them! Jesus Christ made it clear when He encouraged His disciples to "permit the children to come to Him, and not hinder them, for God's kingdom is theirs.! When children came to Him, He took them in His arms, and began blessing them, laying His hands on them. (Mark 10:14 and 16) Obviously Jesus Christ has great regard for the little ones, as well as desires for them to get to <u>know</u> Him! In my office, when serving as the Children's Pastor, I had several pictures of such depictions. Of Jesus holding and laughing with children. Imagine the star maker, taking great delight in the "Wee Masterpieces" He holds so dear.

Thank you for choosing to plant seeds of truth,
in God's tender garden...a child!

1st Commandment: Since God made everything you see....yes, STOP, look around. Count every thing you see! And when you've counted, remember, God made each of them for our good. Sun for warmth and daylight, plants for food, and that make the air we breathe. Birds to sing beautiful songs and see all those wonderful colors? Dogs to be our friends and protectors, green grass to lay in and watch clouds go by, that bring rain so all of us have a drink! God is the smartest, most thoughtful and only Creator. He deserves to be our only God!!!

2nd Commandment: People look at all the beautiful "things" God made, and decide to pray to the "thing". They forget God. So they put a star on a pole and sing to it, pray to it for rain, bring it prizes. Or, maybe, it's something else God made and they make a statue of it, and even though it can't see, can't hear, or love them back, they get fooled by the devil to pray to it, and they worship the statue of wood, or stone they have carved. Don't they know, THAT'S NOT GOD? It's an idol! God wants us to have only Him as our God!

3rd Commandment: Sometimes we say words without thinking. Or if we get angry, we blame God for our trouble. We hear people say "God", but they aren't praying to Him. Or they use God's name to show off or try to scare others, but they don't love God, or else they wouldn't hurt His holy name like that. Be careful to only say His name when you're talking or singing to Him, He loves that!

9

4ᵗʰ Commandment: The Sabbath day is the one day of the week we celebrate all day, the things God has helped us with. We rest from all work so we can think about God and all the good things He has done ever since He made the world and all the people. Amazing miracles, (which are mighty things only God can do), like making a dry path right through the middle of the sea! So dry people could walk on it! Maybe He helped your mom or dad get extra money for a vacation. Or healed someone you love from a bad sickness. You know if we stop and think about it, we could sing songs of praise to Him all day for all the ways He shows us His love. He even sings over you at night when you are fast asleep! He enjoys when we go to church and learn about Him. The temptation to do other things rather than go to church, is always calling us, but don't listen. Just go to church, read your Bible, and listen to His words. That's keeping the Sabbath holy!

5th Commandment: Parents deserve our respect by not talking back, helping them with chores, making a nice thank you card, but especially, when we obey them when we don't really want to! Do right by them even when they don't deserve it...by cheering them up when they're having a bad day. Be good, so your parents are proud of you! Look for ways to make them happy. God wants you to honor them!

6ᵗʰ Commandment: Video games, T.V., and bad music often teach us to destroy others, by planning an attack on them, to kill them! This is not God's way! He wants us to love others the way He does. When they slap us on one cheek, we turn the other cheek as if to say, even if you hurt me, I'll love you for God's sake! It's hard to do, but if we practice forgiveness, we will never <u>plan</u> out to kill anyone.

7ᵗʰ Commandment: Have you ever been to a wedding? Where a man and a woman make a promise to God and to each other, to love and take care of each other until they die? That's God's way! But the devil tempts husbands to find a new wife because he forgot his promise to God. Or, the wife forgets her promise and says.. "I'm going to find a new husband. I'm tired of the old one." But it would be better to make sure you mean it when you make a promise to God! Make sure you really, really love each other... for keeps! Then have a wedding before God, and promise Him you'll be true to your mate. God will help with a lifetime of marriage!

8th Commandment: Once when I was small, I went to the grocery store with my mom. She was paying the cashier for the groceries, when all of a sudden, there it was…a candy bar! And chocolate! I looked to see if Mom was watching me. She wasn't! And while no one else was watching, I took that candy bar and hid it in my pocket . When we got in the car I could hardly wait to eat it. So, I opened it and before I could get a bite, Mom heard the candy wrapper unfolding, turned around and asked me where I got it? I couldn't think of a good answer, so she marched me and the candy bar right back to the store manager, and made me say I was sorry for stealing it! I was so ashamed, I never did **that** again! I worked for money so I could pay for what I wanted. That's God's way!

9th Commandment: To accuse someone of something wrong, when you know they didn't do it, is being a false, untrue, witness. Once, a girl looked over on my test, to get the answers. She didn't want to study, it was too much work. But she wanted to pass the test. She thought the easy way was to write down <u>my</u> answers. When I looked at her, she yelled for the teacher and said <u>I</u> was cheating! That was not true…she was a false witness! Sometimes others want us to take sides, so to be their friend, we lie for them. That's NOT God's way. Don't be a false witness!

10th Commandment: Did you know God will take care of us and give us everything we need, if we t<u>rust</u> Him? When we ask God to bless our food, and make it good for our bodies…He does! But oh, oh. We see our friends with a new bike, we want it! Or if they have a new game…we want it! Maybe they have their own room in a big house, or a swimming pool or a stick horse, or a real horse… we want that! But the trouble is, when that's all we think about, we believe "I've got to <u>have</u> it! I've GOT to have it!" We're NOT believing God will care for us. We don't care about anyone else! We don't need it, but want it so bad, we talk ourselves into thinking we have to have it! That's not trusting God, but ourselves! If we really needed it, 'God would provide it. How do I know? God said so! And I've learned when God says something, He means it! He never lies but only tells the truth. So if He said it, it's as good as a promise! So don't covet what your neighbors have, be satisfied with what you have and thank God!

ABOUT THE AUTHOR:

Maureen T. McGinn has loved and worked with children for over 40 years, as a Children's Pastor for 10 years, through VBS's, backyard bible clubs and all variety of venues, Sharing the significant truths of God's word in creative ways in order to convey God's truth to children early in their life.

Printed in the United States
by Baker & Taylor Publisher Services